LAUBACH WAY TO
Reading 4

A time-tested method that has taught millions of adults to read

PEOPLE AND PLACES

FRANK C. LAUBACH • ELIZABETH MOONEY KIRK • ROBERT S. LAUBACH

CAROLINE BLAKELY

LINGUISTIC CONSULTANT: JEANETTE D. MACERO

New Readers Press
ProLiteracy's publishing division

People and Places
ISBN 978-1-56420-928-3

Copyright © 2011, 1991, 1984 New Readers Press
New Readers Press
ProLiteracy's Publishing Division
104 Marcellus Street, Syracuse, New York 13204
www.newreaderspress.com

Printed in the United States of America
9 8 7 6 5 4 3

Proceeds from the sale of New Readers Press materials support professional development, training, and technical assistance programs of ProLiteracy that benefit local literacy programs in the U.S. and around the globe.

Developmental Editor: Terrie Lipke
Creative Director: Andrea Woodbury
Production Specialist: Maryellen Casey
Art and Design Supervisor: James P. Wallace
Illustrations: Luigi Galante, represented by Wilkinson Studios, Inc.
Cover Design: Carolyn Wallace

Contents

Maps

North America

Alaska (UNITED STATES)

British Columbia

CANADA

Newfoundland

Quebec

Vancouver

Ontario

St. John's

Fort Clatsop

Thunder Bay

North Dakota

South Dakota

New York

Iowa

Pacific Ocean

California

UNITED STATES

Missouri

Kansas

St. Louis

Washington, D.C.

Arkansas

Alabama

Atlantic Ocean

Tuskegee

Texas

Mississippi

Florida

CUBA

MEXICO

0   500   1000   1500   2000

Scale of miles

5

George Washington Carver

George Washington Carver
From Slave to Scientist

Carver	Missouri (Mi zuur' ē)
death (deth)	peanut
famous (fā' mus)	scientist (sī' en tist)
George (Jorj)	slave
hungry	southwest
known	tiny

The tiny slave baby was cold and hungry. He coughed and then began to cry. Night riders had taken him and his mother off into the dark night.

The time was 1864 during the Civil War. The place was the Carver farm in southwest Missouri. Night riders rode across the state and stole slaves to sell in Texas.

The baby's mother was the Carvers' only slave. Farmer Carver tried to get the mother and baby back. He offered the night riders his best horse for them. The night riders took the horse, but left only the tiny baby. His mother was never heard of again.

The baby was called George. The farmer's wife added Washington to that. And, since slaves took their owner's last name, the baby's full name was George Washington Carver. Looking at the tiny, sickly baby, Farmer Carver said, "He may die before morning. I didn't get much for my best horse."

Time would tell that the farmer's words were not true. The tiny slave baby grew up to become a famous scientist. Today, more than 60 years after his death, George Washington Carver is still one of the best-known black Americans. Most people still remember him as the "Peanut Man."

7

Getting an Education

The Carvers were middle-aged and had no children. They took in the baby and were the only parents George ever knew. Because the boy was small and sickly, he could not help with the plowing or other heavy farm work. He stayed in the house and learned to cook and wash clothes. Later, these skills helped him get through school.

George liked gardening better than anything else. He brought wild flowers from the woods and planted them in his own garden. These plants took the place of toys and friends. George loved the flowers and talked to them. They grew better for him than for anyone else. Neighbors started calling George the "plant doctor."

The Carvers saw that this boy was bright. But he could not go to school in the neighborhood. Although slaves became free after the Civil War, black and white children were not allowed to go to school together where he lived. The nearest school for blacks was in a town eight miles away.

When George was about 12 years old, he told the Carvers that he would like to live in town and go to school. The Carvers said he could go, but he would have to be on his own. So, with nothing but the clothes he wore and one dollar, the boy left the only home he had ever known. He walked the eight miles to town to start school.

agriculture (ag' ri cul chur)	Simpson
degree	soil
Iowa (Ī' u wu)	

At first, George slept in a barn near town. Sometimes he was hungry. Then a friendly black woman took him in. "It's high time some of your own kind helped to raise you," she told George. She did laundry for white people, and George helped her. She also taught him to make medicine from roots and leaves of plants.

After three years, George left Missouri to go to Kansas. He thought he could get a better education there. He got jobs as a cook or gardener to pay his way while he went to school. When he was 22, George graduated with honors from a high school in Kansas. He was making plans to go to a college in that state. Those plans ended when the college president saw that George was black and refused to admit him.

For the next three years, young George Carver lived alone on a farm in a little house with a dirt floor. The land was poor. He had a hard time raising crops. During this time, George made up his mind to go to college and learn ways to raise crops on poor soil.

First, George went to Simpson College, a small college in Iowa. Then, he went to Iowa State University. This school was known for its teaching of agriculture and plant science. George had decided to become a plant scientist. He graduated from Iowa State and stayed on for two years, teaching and working on a higher degree. He was also looking for God's plan for his life.

9

Places in
George Washington Carver's Life

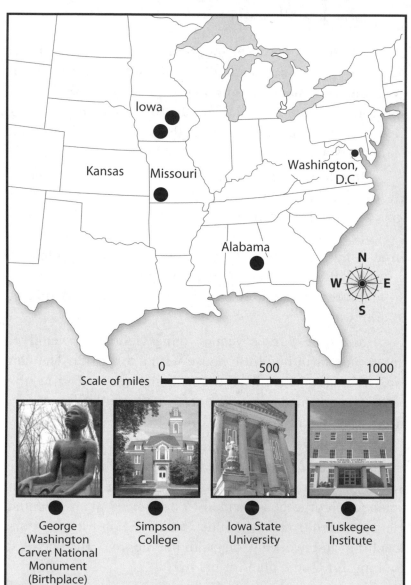

Iowa

Kansas   Missouri

Washington,
D.C.

Alabama

N
W   E
S

0   500   1000
Scale of miles

George
Washington
Carver National
Monument
(Birthplace)

Simpson
College

Iowa State
University

Tuskegee
Institute

Booker	science (sī' ence)
greenhouse	special (spesh' ul)
institute	Tuskegee (Tus kē' gee)
professor	

Even as a young man, George Washington Carver always felt that God had something special for him to do with his life. He didn't know what it might be because he was good at music and painting as well as science.

In 1896, he got a letter from the president of Tuskegee Institute in Alabama. This school had been started to teach skills to freed slaves. Now, it was planning a new department of agriculture.

"We need you to head the department," Dr. Booker T. Washington wrote to George Carver. "I can't afford to make you rich or famous. I can offer you nothing but hard work and the chance to help our hungry people. You can teach them how to raise the food they need."

George Carver felt that this was God's special plan for his life. "I will come," he wrote back.

Teaching at Tuskegee

At Iowa State, the young professor had a fine lab and greenhouse, but things were very different at Tuskegee Institute. There was no lab or greenhouse. There were hardly any plants at the school, and the land was poor. For too long, cotton had been the only crop in Alabama. Cotton had used up the plant food in the soil.

In addition to these problems, there were few students who wanted to study farming. Most of the students had grown up on poor farms. They were at school to get away from the farm. They wanted to learn skills to make money.

11

Professor Carver works in his lab at Tuskegee.

acre (ā' ker)	material
boll (bōll)	rotate (rō' tate)
cookstove	sweet
improve	weevil

Professor Carver used what was at hand to overcome his problems. He and his students looked in trash cans to find pans, jars, and anything to cook with. These went into the lab for what Professor Carver called his "cookstove chemistry."

Tuskegee Institute gave its new department of agriculture 19 acres of no-good land. With poor land and a lab made from trash, George Carver began showing farmers what science could do for farming.

First, Professor Carver showed the farmers how to improve their soil. He and his students brought mud and leaves from the bottom land near the river. They plowed this material into the soil along with animal droppings from the barns.

Then, the professor told the farmers that cotton was taking the plant food out of their soil. "If you plant other crops like peanuts, beans, and sweet potatoes, you'll make the soil good again," he said.

"If you want to improve your soil, you must rotate the crops. Besides, it is not safe to plant only cotton. What if the boll weevil comes and kills your cotton? Then you'll have nothing to sell. You should plant some food crops so that you'll never go hungry."

At first, the people laughed at George Carver. "What can a college professor from the North know about cotton?" they asked. But when they saw that his farm grew more cotton than theirs because he rotated crops, they stopped laughing. Professor Carver got 500 pounds of cotton from each acre. "No one else ever got that much cotton from this land," the farmers admitted.

Some of the farmers knew then that Professor Carver was right. They began to rotate their crops. They planted a crop of sweet potatoes that was followed by a crop of peanuts. After that, they planted cotton. And that cotton crop was the best they had seen in years.

13

Professor Carver studies plants.

But many of the farmers still planted too much cotton and too few other crops. Then an insect called the boll weevil came to Alabama. The boll weevils killed the cotton almost overnight. The farmers who had planted only cotton were left without money or food.

Because they were afraid to plant cotton, many of the farmers planted peanuts. Professor Carver had said that peanuts could be used for many things. The farms for miles around had acres and acres of peanuts. Peanuts filled the barns. Peanuts lay on the ground. "Who is going to buy our peanuts?" the farmers asked.

The people in the North had all the peanuts they wanted. Professor Carver had told the farmers different ways to use peanuts for food. But the farmers wanted more than food. They were hungry for money. They were angry at the professor from Tuskegee.

George Carver saw that he had saved the people from one problem but had caused another. The people were no longer killing their soil with cotton. But he had told them to plant a crop they couldn't sell. They had a right to be angry.

When George Carver had a problem, he often asked God for the answer. Now, he asked God, "You made the peanut. What can it be used for?"

He believed he heard God's answer. "I've given you some peanuts and a good head. Take the peanuts into the lab and pull them apart."

15

| invent | product | use (ūs) |
| pecan (pi con') | rest | |

So Professor Carver took bags of peanuts into his lab and locked the door. In the next six days, he mixed the different parts of the peanut in many different ways. He found that peanut oil could be made into a kind of butter and a cooking oil.

Then he turned to the dry part of the peanut that was left after the oil was taken out. He mixed it with water and put it over a fire. It looked like milk. He took a drink of it. Yes, it could be used for milk!

Professor Carver mixed different things with the peanuts. As the days passed, the jars and pans were filled with many new products. There was fine writing paper and rich plant food for the soil. He also made a hard, shiny material to be used in building houses and other materials for building roads.

When he left his lab, Professor Carver knew that with God's help he could find many uses for the peanut. He knew there would be a market for the farmers' peanuts.

Becoming Famous

George Carver spent the rest of his life finding new ways to use the peanut and telling people about them. In all, he found 300 new uses for the peanut.

He also looked for ways to use sweet potatoes and pecans. These farm products grew well in the South. Professor Carver thought that farmers could sell them if people knew how to use them. In his lab at Tuskegee, George Carver invented 118 products from the sweet potato. From pecans, he made 75 products.

16

businessmen	museum (mū zē' um)
Congress	travel

As time went on, factories began to make products like Carver's. Peanuts, pecans, and sweet potatoes became important money crops in the South.

Professor Carver's work with the peanut made him famous. But he also made the peanut famous. In order to sell more peanuts, peanut businessmen printed his story in newspapers and books. There were also radio programs and a movie about him.

In 1921, when Congress was talking about a special tax on peanuts from other countries, Professor Carver was asked to speak. He traveled to Washington, D.C., and spoke before Congress. Although it was very hard for any black person to travel at that time, George Carver went to many colleges and farmers' meetings to speak.

People all over the world heard about George Washington Carver and his work with the peanut. Some people said he had invented a new science called plant chemistry. Simpson College, the small college he went to in Iowa, honored him with a doctor's degree. Another university in New York honored him with a doctor's degree. He got job offers that would have paid a lot of money. But he stayed at Tuskegee for the rest of his life.

Before his death in 1943, the George Washington Carver Museum was opened at Tuskegee Institute. Today, people travel to Tuskegee to visit the museum. They see almost a thousand products that George Carver invented. Also in the museum are his paintings. He painted most of these pictures with paint he made from Alabama soil.

17

birthplace	monument

After his death, an act of Congress made a national monument of George Washington Carver's birthplace. The monument covers 210 acres of the farm in southwest Missouri where he was born as a slave. A sign says, Birthplace of George Washington Carver, Great Scientist.

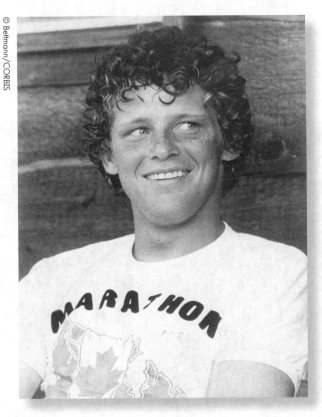

Terry Fox
Marathon of Hope

artificial (ar ti fi' shul)	marathon
Atlantic	ocean (ō' shun)
dip	Pacific
Fox	Terry

Terry Fox dipped his right leg into the cold water of the Atlantic Ocean. But he didn't feel the cold. His right leg was artificial.

He was thinking, "Before long, I'll be dipping my leg into the Pacific Ocean on the other side of Canada."

Terry Fox runs on his Marathon of Hope across Canada.

British	hop
Columbia	painful
Newfoundland (New' fund lund)	province
research (rē' serch)	skip
St. (Saint)	toward (tord)
Vancouver (Van coo' ver)	twist

Terry Fox pulled his artificial leg out of the cold Atlantic. He began to run toward the west. The Marathon of Hope had started. It was April, 1980. Terry was running across Canada to raise money for cancer research.

The young man's running was painful to watch. First, he would twist his body to throw his artificial leg ahead of him. Then he took a step, and a hop, and a skip. Twist, step, hop, skip. Slowly and painfully, Terry Fox began his run.

Each day, he woke up at 4 a.m. By 5 o'clock, he was out on the road, running. Twist, step, hop, skip. Some days, he ran 26 miles. A marathon is 26 miles. Terry was trying to run a marathon each day all the way across Canada.

Terry Fox started his run near St. John's in the province of Newfoundland. He was running toward his home in Vancouver, British Columbia, almost 5,000 miles away.

But Terry didn't take the shortest way east to west from St. John's to Vancouver. He wanted to run where people could see him. So he avoided the big highways between cities and took longer roads that went through small towns.

21

Canadian	exact	horn
cheer	honk	inspire

At each town, the people came out to cheer him on. Many shouted, "Go, Terry, go!" Sometimes, people joined Terry and ran a few miles with him to cheer him on. As drivers passed him on the road, they honked their horns to cheer him on.

Each day, the newspapers and television stations told the people where Terry Fox would run. Radio stations played a record, "Run, Terry, Run!" Every day, more and more people lined up along the road to cheer him on.

Terry Fox's Marathon of Hope inspired people everywhere who were in pain. His run brought all Canadians together. One newspaper wrote, "Canadians are many different people, with different ideas. But on one thing we agree. We cheer on this young man who is so full of courage. His run across Canada is like a zipper bringing Canadians together."

* * *

Terry Fox was born near Vancouver, British Columbia. When he was a teenager, he was a good basketball player and a fast runner. He went to the university to study how the human body works. He wanted to learn exactly how the legs and arms work so that he could teach other runners.

hospital	real	treat
outlook	society (so cī' e ty)	treatment

In 1977, doctors found cancer in Terry's right leg. They had to take his leg off above the knee. For 18 months, Terry stayed at home or in the hospital, taking treatment for the cancer. The cancer treatment made him sick and made his hair fall out. Terry felt very sorry for himself. The treatment hurt a lot. But his feelings about himself hurt even more.

Two things happened to Terry to help him change his outlook on life. He read in the paper about a man with one leg who was running in the New York Marathon. That inspired Terry to say, "If that man can run, I can, too!"

Terry visited people being treated in a cancer hospital. "Some of them showed real courage," Terry said. "But others had given up smiling. I decided to do all that my body could do. I would push myself to the limit. Somewhere the hurting must stop."

Terry Fox decided to run across Canada. First, he went into training. He trained for 14 months. The first few days, he could run only a mile a day. But he added more and more each day until he was running 26 miles a day. "I ran exactly 3,419 miles during my training," Terry said. "I know, because I kept a daily record."

While Terry was in training, he asked the people of Canada to give money for cancer research. Then, as he began running toward the west, the money began coming in for the Canadian Cancer Society.

23

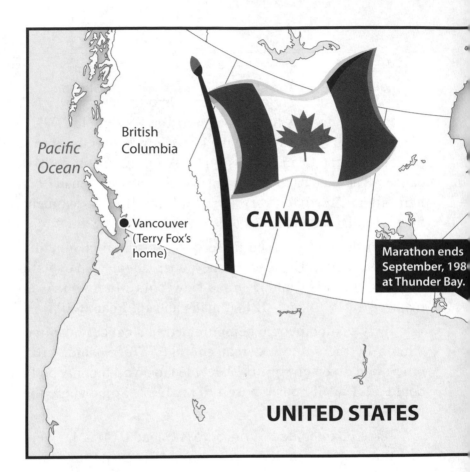

Pacific
Ocean

British
Columbia

● Vancouver
(Terry Fox's
home)

CANADA

Marathon ends
September, 198
at Thunder Bay.

UNITED STATES

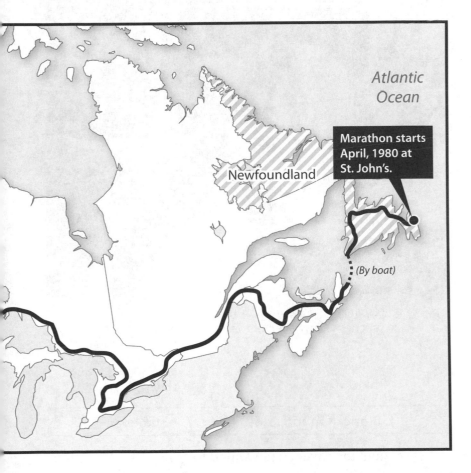

Atlantic Ocean

Newfoundland

Marathon starts April, 1980 at St. John's.

(By boat)

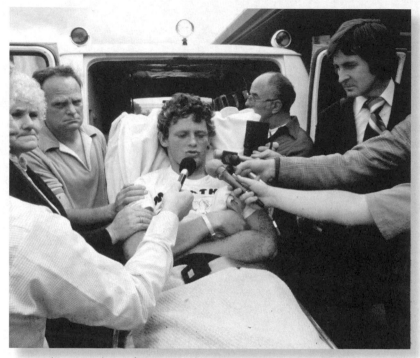

As the Marathon of Hope ends in Thunder Bay, Terry Fox speaks to reporters. On the left are Terry's mother and father.

Ontario (On tār' ē ō)	Quebec

It seemed that everyone wanted to give to the Marathon of Hope. School children sold cookies to raise money. Baseball fans took up money at games. Churches held bake sales. TV stations raised money. The government voted money for cancer research.

Terry Fox kept running, through the provinces on the Atlantic Ocean, then through Quebec, and into Ontario. Everywhere, the people cheered him on. Drivers honked their horns. Money kept coming in for the Cancer Society.

bay	lung	weak
halfway	thunder	whole (hole)

The many miles of running each day hurt Terry more and more. In Quebec, he began getting weaker. As he ran into Ontario, his lungs hurt, and he got weaker and weaker.

By the first day of September, almost five months after the Marathon of Hope began, Terry was near Thunder Bay, Ontario. He felt that he could run no more. He was coughing and choking and was in great pain. But there were people ahead, waving and cheering and honking their horns. "There was no way I was going to stop running," Terry said. "Not with all those people watching."

Later that day, when the people were behind him, Terry had to stop. The pain in his lungs was more than he could stand. The Marathon of Hope had ended.

Terry was taken to a hospital in Thunder Bay. Doctors found that the cancer was now in his lungs. He had to fly home to Vancouver for hospital treatment.

Terry Fox had run through the provinces on the Atlantic, through Quebec, and through part of Ontario. He had run exactly 3,339 miles. He had run only halfway across the nation. But, as one newspaper reporter wrote, "Terry Fox pulled the whole nation together."

At home, Terry knew that his Marathon of Hope was still inspiring all of Canada. The money for cancer research kept coming in. In all, the Cancer Society got $24 million. That was a dollar for every man, woman, and child in Canada.

27

Marathon of Hope

Terry Fox

30

Canada

Marathon de l'espoir

Above, Terry receives the Order of
Canada, his country's highest honor.
Right, a Canadian postage stamp
honors Terry Fox and his Marathon of Hope.

| hero | postage | spirit | stamp |

The government gave Terry Fox its highest honor, the Order of Canada. A postage stamp honored the Marathon of Hope. This postage stamp showed Terry Fox on his run. It was the first time that a Canadian postage stamp honored a person who was still living.

Terry got weaker, and he had more and more pain. But he had a happy spirit. He told funny stories when friends came to visit him. He didn't show them that he was in pain.

One day, Terry read a newspaper headline, "Cancer Beats Runner." He told his friends, "That paper is all wrong. Maybe cancer beat my body, but it couldn't touch my spirit. The spirit is more important than the body."

Terry Fox died on June 28, 1981. He was only 22 years old. At the time of his death, many people spoke of his courage. One young woman seemed to speak for the whole nation. "Canada needs heroes. Terry Fox was a real hero. He was a real Canadian hero."

Sacajawea
Across the Shining Mountains

buffalo	Charbonneau (Shar bon ō')
captain	Clark
French	Dakota (Du kō' tu)
trade	Mandan
village	Sacajawea (Sac' u ju wē' u)
	Shoshoni (Shō shō' nē)

This true story happened many years ago when buffalo covered the land in what is now North Dakota. White men came to the Mandan Indian village on the Missouri River. Captain Lewis was one of their leaders. Captain Clark was the other. The men spent the winter in the village, getting ready to go on to the Pacific Ocean.

"We will never get across the Rocky Mountains without help," said Captain Clark. "Shoshoni Indians live there. We need them to help us find horses and a guide. But they do not trust white men."

"Sacajawea is a Shoshoni," said Captain Lewis. "She is the wife of Charbonneau, the French trader from Canada. Charbonneau knows some Indian languages and wants a job with us. I don't like him, but if his wife comes along, I'll pay him $25 a month."

30

chief (chēf)	fell	fork

Charbonneau brought his 16-year-old wife to talk with Lewis and Clark. Sacajawea was small, but strong. Her long black hair was parted in the middle. It fell in two thick ropes across her chest. Her eyes lighted up as the men talked about her people.

"I know Shoshoni country," Sacajawea said. "Take me to Three Forks. That is where three rivers come together to form the Missouri River. From there, I will take you to the Shoshonis. My father was a great Shoshoni chief. The Shoshonis will welcome us." She was speaking in the Shoshoni language, so Charbonneau had to tell Lewis and Clark what she was saying. The captains felt sure Sacajawea could help them get through Shoshoni country.

The name Sacajawea means Bird Woman. Sacajawea was born in the Rocky Mountains, which the Indians called the Shining Mountains. When she was about 12, an enemy war party killed her parents and took her as a slave. These Indians carried her far away from Shoshoni country.

Charbonneau traded with the Indians who held Sacajawea as a slave. When he saw the girl, he wanted her for his wife and traded a white buffalo skin for her. The French trader brought her to the Mandan village on the Missouri River where Lewis and Clark found them. That was in the fall of 1804.

31

The United States in 1803

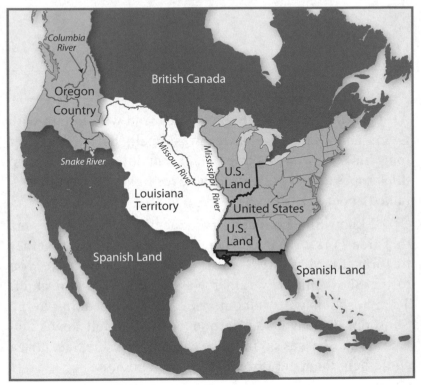

Columbia
River

British Canada

Oregon
Country

Snake River

Missouri River

Mississippi River

U.S.
Land

Louisiana
Territory

United States

U.S.
Land

Spanish Land

Spanish Land

canoe (cu noo')	Mississippi
cross	set
explore	territory
Jefferson	Thomas (Tom' us)
Louis (Loo' is)	unfriendly
Louisiana (Loo ē' zē an' u)	

The Louisiana Territory

The year before, in 1803, President Thomas Jefferson had bought the Louisiana Territory from France. This land reached from the Mississippi River to the Rocky Mountains. White men had never set foot on most of it. It was a huge, wild country. Indians, both friendly and unfriendly, lived there.

The United States was a young nation then and not very big or strong. Thomas Jefferson was the third president. He dreamed of having the United States reach from the Atlantic Ocean to the Pacific Ocean.

Congress was not as excited about the big, wild country as Jefferson was. Congress voted only $2,500 to pay for exploring the country.

President Jefferson picked Captain Lewis and Captain Clark to explore the Louisiana Territory. They planned to travel up the Mississippi River to St. Louis and then up the Missouri River to Dakota country. Their idea was to follow the Missouri River to where it started in the Rocky Mountains. Then they planned to cross the mountains by horseback. When they reached a river running west, they planned to continue to the Pacific Ocean by canoe.

33

berry	fort
built (bilt)	row (rōw)
cradle	rowboat
expedition	

The Lewis and Clark Expedition, as it was called, left St. Louis in May of 1804 and started up the Missouri River. In October, the explorers reached the Mandan village where Sacajawea and Charbonneau lived. The Mandans were friendly Indians, so the exploring party built a fort and stayed all winter.

In February of 1805, Sacajawea gave birth to a son. She made a beautiful cradle board to carry him on her back.

Sacajawea Joins the Expedition

In April of 1805, the expedition set out again. The 30 explorers were joined by Sacajawea, her husband Charbonneau, and their two-month-old baby. The party was traveling in two big rowboats. By day, the men rowed up the Missouri River against the fast-moving water. At night, they camped on the shore. Buffalo and other wild animals were everywhere, so the explorers had a lot of fresh meat to eat.

As they traveled, Sacajawea did much to make life easier for the men. With her baby in the cradle board on her back, she looked for roots and berries. She had learned from her grandmother which plants were safe to eat and which were not. The roots and berries were a welcome addition to the all-meat menu.

34

equipment	steep	waterfall
	storm	

Sacajawea also sewed clothes for the men and caught fish for their meals. She warned the men of waterfalls and other dangers they would come to. She began learning English so that she could talk to them. She helped the explorers make friends with Indians along the way.

One afternoon, while the men were on the shore, a great storm came up. The wind caused one of the rowboats to turn over on its side. Medicines, important papers, and equipment fell into the water. Charbonneau was in the boat, but he didn't know what to do. Sacajawea, with her baby on her back, jumped into the icy water. She rescued most of the equipment and other things. Captain Clark told Sacajawea, "You saved the expedition."

The party came to a great waterfall on the Missouri River and had to carry their boats and equipment around it. Clark, Charbonneau, and Sacajawea were walking on the low ground between the two steep banks when another storm came up. Heavy rains caused a great wall of mud and water to start down the valley toward them. Charbonneau climbed up the steep bank to safety. But the ground was too wet for Sacajawea to climb with the cradle board on her back. Clark got below her and pushed.

The water got higher and higher. It was up to Clark's chest by the time he pushed Sacajawea up the bank. Then he hurried up after her. "Chief Red Hair saved my life!" Sacajawea said. "Chief Red Hair saved my baby!"

35

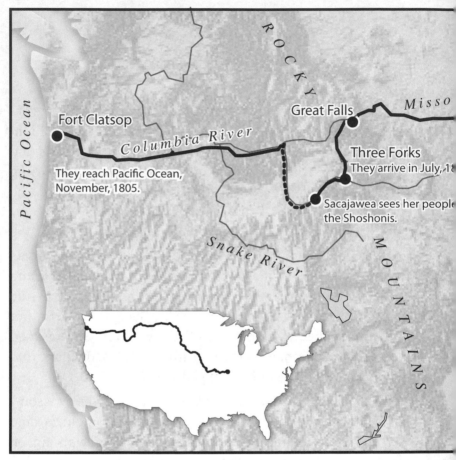

ROCKY

Misso

Great Falls

Fort Clatsop

Columbia River

They reach Pacific Ocean,
November, 1805.

Pacific Ocean

Three Forks
They arrive in July, 1

Sacajawea sees her peopl
the Shoshonis.

Snake River

MOUNTAINS

Clark Expedition

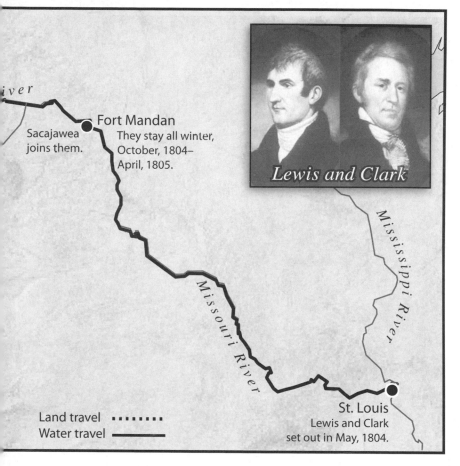

iver

Fort Mandan
They stay all winter,
October, 1804–
April, 1805.

Sacajawea
joins them.

Lewis and Clark

Mississippi River

Missouri River

Land travel ▪▪▪▪▪▪▪▪
Water travel ━━━━━

St. Louis
Lewis and Clark
set out in May, 1804.

A painting shows Sacajawea guiding the explorers.

The exploring party reached Three Forks, the place where three rivers came together to form the Missouri River. Sacajawea said, "I remember this place. I came here with my people on a buffalo hunt. Near here, my parents were killed, and I was stolen."

blanket

The explorers continued up the largest of the three rivers. One day, Sacajawea became very excited. She pointed to a great red rock many miles away. "That rock is not far from the summer camp of my people," she said. "First, we must cross the mountains. There, by a river that runs toward the setting sun, we will find the Shoshonis."

Captain Lewis went ahead to look for the Shoshonis. Sacajawea told him how to show that he was a friend. "Wave a blanket high over your head, and bring it down to the ground. Wave the blanket and bring it down three times," she said.

Lewis came back with some of the Shoshonis. Sacajawea danced for joy. One of them was her brother. She had not seen him for five years, and now he was the chief of the Shoshonis.

Sacajawea and her brother talked. She told him that the explorers wanted horses and a guide. "Can we trust these white men?" her brother asked.

"Yes," said Sacajawea. "I have watched and listened. They do what they say they will do."

So the Shoshoni chief helped the explorers buy horses and find a guide. Even the Indians were afraid to cross the Rocky Mountains. The only guide who could be found was an old man who had crossed the mountains as a boy. Sacajawea did not stay with her people. She went on with the explorers.

39

Crossing the Rocky Mountains

The hardest part of the journey came in the next two months. The group, now on horseback, climbed up, up, up, toward the snow-covered mountain tops. They climbed over rocks and dead trees. They cut their way through thick bushes. Sometimes the way was so steep that the horses fell down.

The explorers went through icy rain and then snow. The winter snows were almost upon them. There were no wild animals, so the food was running out. They used up all of the dried meat and flour. One day, they went without any food at all. "Without food, we will be too weak to go on," said Captain Lewis. He ordered the men to kill a horse, then a second, and a third.

Sacajawea would not eat the meat from the horses. "Shoshonis do not eat an animal that works for them," she said. There were no berries, so she ate the bark off the trees, as the horses did.

At last, they reached the top of a mountain and saw a valley on the other side. It was the first time that white men had crossed the Rocky Mountains.

On the west side of the mountain, the exploring party found friendly Indians. The Indians brought dried fish and roots and told them how to reach the Pacific Ocean. Leaving their horses behind, the explorers built canoes and journeyed down the Snake River. It ran into the Columbia River, which ran into the Pacific Ocean.

On November 7, 1805, the explorers had their first sight of the Pacific Ocean. Captain Clark wrote in his notebook, "Ocean in view! Oh, the joy!"

| Captain Clark | Captain Lewis |

| claim | Clatsop | Oregon (Or' u gon) |

Oregon Country

The land between the Rocky Mountains and the Pacific Ocean was called Oregon Country. At that time, Oregon Country did not belong to any nation. Lewis and Clark claimed Oregon Country for the United States.

The explorers built a fort about a mile from the ocean. They named the fort after Clatsop Indians living near there. The explorers spent the winter at Fort Clatsop. In the spring, they started back home. They went back up the Columbia River, back over the mountains and through Shoshoni country, back down the Missouri River.

It was August of 1806 when the expedition reached the Mandan village on the Missouri River. That was the end of the journey for Sacajawea, Charbonneau, and their baby. The little boy was 19 months old and had traveled almost 7,000 miles on his mother's back.

41

A Place in History

Lewis and Clark were heroes when they got back to St. Louis. Their expedition became a part of U.S. history. They were the first white men to explore the Louisiana Territory and Oregon Country. Other American families followed them and made their homes there. The nation reached from ocean to ocean.

Most of what we know about Sacajawea came from the daily records Lewis and Clark kept while they were traveling. They said she played an important part in the expedition. She not only guided them through Shoshoni country, they said, but she helped them get along with the Indians all along the way. "A woman with a party of men is a sign of peace," Captain Clark wrote in his daily record. To show his thanks for her help, Clark took Sacajawea's son into his home and gave him an education.

There are different stories about Sacajawea's life after the expedition. Some people claim that she died in 1812 in her twenties. Others claim that she lived to be almost 100 years old.

Today, Sacajawea has a special place in American history. There are statues of her in North Dakota, Oregon, and other states. No other American woman has been honored by so many statues.

The statue in Oregon shows a young woman with a baby on her back. She is pointing the way for a nation to follow across the "Shining Mountains."

42

Above, a statue in Oregon shows Sacajawea with her baby on her back. Right, this U.S. dollar coin honors Sacajawea.

Dr. Frank C. Laubach

Frank C. Laubach
Voice of the Silent Billion

belt	Lanao (Lan' ou)
billion (bil' yun)	Laubach (Lou' bok or Law' bok)
dagger	Maranao (Mār' u nou)
flash	Muslim (Muz' lim)
Frank	Philippines (Phil' i pēnz)
island (ī' land)	powerful

Think of a time long ago and a place far away from the United States. The time was 1930. The place was Lanao Province in the Philippines. The Philippines is an island nation in the Pacific Ocean, not far from China.

Among the Maranaos

A small, hot room was crowded with men and women, all dressed in brightly colored clothes. These people were Maranaos. The Maranaos were Muslims who lived on a big island in the south of the Philippines.

An important meeting was ready to start. Two men were sitting at a table at the front of the room. One of the men was a chief of Lanao Province. He was a very powerful chief. You could tell that just by looking at him. This Muslim chief was about five and a half feet tall, with flashing black eyes. A long dagger was in his belt.

literacy (lit' er u cy)   stood
missionary (mish' un ār y)

The other man at the table was only a little taller than the chief. This man was an American missionary. He had light blue eyes and a kind smile. But that day his smile seemed sad.

This missionary was Frank C. Laubach.

The missionary stood up and began to speak. "My friends," Dr. Laubach began in the Maranao language. He was still learning to speak Maranao, so he spoke very slowly.

"My friends," Dr. Laubach said, "with our lessons, thousands of people in Lanao have learned to read and write Maranao. Our teachers have taught them in the market places and in their homes. Now, mothers are reading books about child care. Farmers are reading books about better farming.

"But, my friends," the missionary continued, "I have some sad news for you. There is a great depression in the world. Because of the depression, many people in the United States are out of work. They can't give much money to their missionaries.

"I don't have any more money to pay our teachers," Dr. Laubach said sadly. "Without money, I don't see how our literacy program can continue."

The Philippines
An island nation in the Pacific Ocean

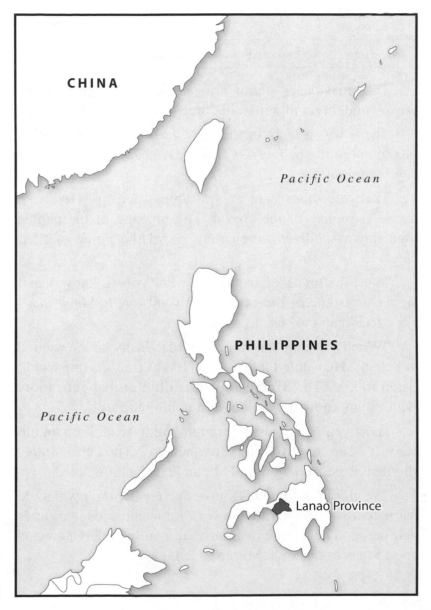

CHINA

Pacific Ocean

PHILIPPINES

Pacific Ocean

Lanao Province

buzz	several	sudden	wipe

The missionary could not speak any longer. He sat down suddenly and wiped his face.

There was a buzz in the crowded room as the people talked about the bad news. The buzzing sound went on for several minutes.

Then the other man at the table stood up. He spoke above the noise of the crowd. The buzzing of the people died down suddenly when they heard the voice of their chief.

The Muslim chief began. "I want you to know that I am a true friend of literacy. And I want you to know that I am a true friend of Dr. Laubach.

"When Dr. Laubach came to Lanao last year, he wanted to help us. He wanted to teach us. But at first, no one would listen to him. The Maranao people did not like education. We did not know how education could help us.

"Last year, Dr. Laubach taught me to read. I am an old man. If I can learn to read, anyone can." The chief almost shouted as he said again, "If I can learn, anyone can!"

The chief continued, "I have been watching my people learn to read and write. Now, I know how education is helping us. The people of Lanao are reading many new and good ideas in our own Maranao language."

48

At center, a Maranao chief of the 1930s welcomes Dr. Laubach.

Then the chief came to the high point in his speech. "Dr. Laubach told us that there is no more money to pay teachers. But we cannot let the literacy program stop. What can we do?"

The crowd buzzed again for a minute as the people asked one another, "What can we do?"

49

excitement	meant (ment)

Then they heard their chief's voice again. He was very excited. "I know what I can do," he said. "I learned to read, and I can teach someone else!"

The chief pulled the dagger out of his belt. He held the dagger high over his head. He shouted, "Let everyone who knows how to read teach someone else! Each one teach one, or die!"

The room became very quiet. Then suddenly everyone stood and began to shout with excitement.

"Yes!" they shouted. "There is no money to pay teachers. Let everyone who can read become a teacher without pay. Each one teach one!"

And that is how Each One Teach One began, more than 70 years ago in the Philippines.

No one in Lanao died because he did not teach. But many hundreds of new readers became teachers. A man would teach his wife. The wife would teach her son. Brother would teach brother. Sister would teach sister.

Each One Teach One was a new idea in education. It began with Frank Laubach and his Muslim friends.

What did Each One Teach One mean to the Maranao people? It meant hope. To the men and women of Lanao, it meant hope for a better life.

One man said, "Before Dr. Laubach came to Lanao, I was like a blind man. I could not see because I could not read."

literate (lit' er ut)   pray   prison   ship

Another man said, "I was like a prisoner in jail. I could not break free to a better life because I could not read."

A woman said, "A new life has opened up to me since I learned to read and write."

Around the World

Missionaries in several other islands of the Philippines heard about the literacy program in Lanao. They asked Dr. Laubach to help write books to teach people in those languages, also. The Maranaos were proud that their program was helping others in the Philippines to become literate.

A group of young educated Maranaos wrote a letter. In this letter, they told about Each One Teach One in Lanao. They told what literacy meant to their people.

These young Maranaos sent their letter to kings and queens and presidents of many countries around the world. Soon, many letters came back asking Dr. Laubach to come to help in their countries.

The Maranaos told their missionary friend, "Dr. Laubach, we would like you to stay in Lanao, but the world is calling for your help."

One day in 1935, a big crowd of Maranao chiefs and their followers went down to the ocean. They went to the ship to say good-by. Dr. Laubach's Muslim friends prayed for his safe travel. "Good-by," they said. "Come back soon." They kept waving until the ship was out of sight.

51

Dr. Laubach teaches people how to read in a marketplace of Lanao Province.

Europe (Yuur' up)   international (inter national)

Frank C. Laubach was now an international missionary. During the next 35 years, he traveled to more than 100 countries in Asia, Africa, North America, South America, and Europe. He helped start Each One Teach One literacy programs in more than 300 languages.

52

apostle (u pos' ul)	magazine (mag u zēn')
Bible	simple
illiterate (il literate)	useful

To make lessons in a language, Dr. Laubach worked with a small group of people who knew the language. Together, they wrote charts that showed the sounds and letters of the language. They wrote simple stories that would be interesting and useful to adults in that country. Dr. Laubach trained teachers, writers, and leaders for the new literacy programs.

A magazine writer called Frank Laubach the "Apostle to the Illiterates." An apostle is a person who travels to far countries to bring good news to people. Dr. Laubach brought the good news of literacy to millions of people around the world.

The apostles in the Bible lived a simple life. Frank Laubach and his wife lived a very simple life, too. They lived in a small apartment. They traveled second class by ship or airplane. They were often guests in people's homes. The money they saved by living simply taught more people to read.

Dr. Laubach often met with leaders of a country. He showed them how their people could learn to read. But Dr. Laubach was always happiest when he was teaching a man or a woman. As he taught, he prayed that literacy would open up a new life for his student. He loved the illiterates of the world.

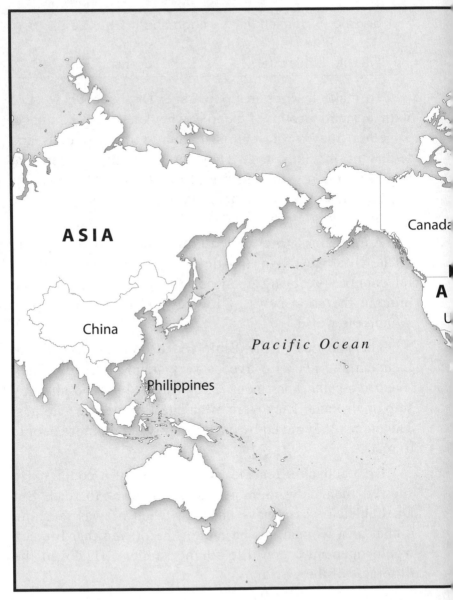

ASIA

China

Philippines

Canada

A

U

Pacific Ocean

World

EUROPE

TH
ICA

tates

Atlantic Ocean

AFRICA

SOUTH
AMERICA

No one knows for sure how many people have learned to read by Each One Teach One. In 1949, *Life* magazine said that more than 60 million people had become literate. Millions more have learned to read since then.

Today, many thousands of teachers are still inspired by the Apostle to the Illiterates. Like the Maranaos, they teach without pay. Like Frank Laubach, they believe that literacy will open up a new life for their students.

His Inner Strength

To really know Frank Laubach, you have to know what he did in the middle of the night. Most of us sleep all night. But Frank Laubach usually woke up about two o'clock in the morning. For two hours, he would pray and read the Bible. These hours in prayer, night after night, made Frank Laubach feel that God was always with him.

Every night, along with his prayer and Bible reading, Frank Laubach wrote a page or two. Over the years, mostly in the middle of the night, he wrote more than 50 books. He wrote books about his work with illiterates and about his life with God.

One of Frank Laubach's books was called *The Game with Minutes*. Once each minute, Frank Laubach tried to remember God. Then, when he looked at someone or thought of someone, he flashed a quick prayer. He flashed a prayer of love to the other person.

Dr. Laubach teaches in an African village.

forgot

Frank Laubach tried to play this "game with minutes" with God every day, even when he was very busy. His game with minutes and his prayer in the middle of the night brought him inner peace and strength.

Frank Laubach spoke in a quiet voice. But his words were full of strength and truth. When people heard him speak in public, they never forgot him. Maybe they forgot his exact words, but they remembered his love for the illiterates of the world.

Dr. Laubach holds a globe showing parts of
the world with many illiterate people.

| earn (ern) | helpless |
| globe | tear (tēr) |

Waking Up America

Frank Laubach made hundreds of public speeches. He spoke in almost every city in the United States and Canada.

"The illiterates of the world are poor and helpless," he told the people of North America. "They earn only a few dollars each year. They can't earn more because they can't read."

In many speeches, Frank Laubach held up a big globe showing the world. The globe had black and white stripes over many countries. Most of these countries were in Africa, Asia, and South America. A few countries were in North America and Europe. Dr. Laubach pointed to the countries under the black and white stripes. "Here is where you will find the people who are poor, sick, and hungry," he said. "And here also is where you will find the illiterates of the world."

Tears filled his eyes as he said, "The children of illiterates die young. Mothers and fathers don't know how to care for their babies' health. Men and women can't grow better crops or get good jobs. That's all because they can't read."

Then he wiped the tears from his eyes. The people listening to him were almost in tears, too. Frank Laubach continued his speech:

"These illiterate men and women around the globe are like people who cannot speak. They have no voice in their government. They cannot write to their leaders. They cannot tell about their needs.

59

Dr. Laubach shows reading charts for an Asian language.

"The illiterates of the world are the silent prisoners of their illiteracy. We can't hear them cry out. We don't know that they are in pain."

About one third of the people of the world were illiterate. Because there were so many of them, Frank Laubach called them the "silent billion." He wrote a book about his life and work called *Forty Years with the Silent Billion*.

Dr. Laubach used his quiet voice and his inner strength to wake up the people of America. Americans, who have so much, learned about the "silent billion," who have so little. Frank Laubach was the voice of the silent billion.

When Frank Laubach died in 1970, he was almost 86 years old. In the last year of his life, he was still making many speeches, writing books, and traveling around the world.

Today, newspapers and magazines continue to write about literacy. Radio and television stations show us the problems of illiteracy around the globe, as well as in the United States and Canada.

There are still almost a billion illiterates in the world. But many groups have heard of their needs and are helping them now. The United Nations teaches illiterates. Governments have literacy programs. Thousands of men and women are learning to read through ProLiteracy, a group that grew out of Frank C. Laubach's work. This international group has literacy programs in the United States and many other countries. Laubach Literacy of Canada helps Canadian adults learn to read.

Students and teachers are still inspired by Frank Laubach and the words of his friend, the Maranao chief:

"If I can learn, anyone can.
If I can teach, anyone can."

Dr. Frank Laubach helped start literacy programs in more than 100 countries and 300 languages. *Laubach Way to Reading* is a set of books Dr. Laubach and others started writing in 1945. Since then, these books have helped millions of people—like you—learn to read better.

Word List

People and Places, the correlated reader for *Laubach Way to Reading 4*, introduces the 174 words listed below. Variants formed by adding *-s, -es, -'s, -s', -ed, -ing, -er, -est, -y,* and *-ly* to previously taught words are not listed, even when *y* is changed to *i* before an ending. New words are listed in their root form when they are used with these previously taught endings.

Word	Page	Word	Page
acre	12	cheer	22
agriculture	9	chief	31
apart	15	claim	41
apostle	53	Clark	30
artificial	19	Clatsop	41
Atlantic	19	Columbia	21
bay	27	Congress	17
belt	45	cookstove	12
berry	34	cradle	34
Bible	53	cross	33
billion	45	dagger	45
birthplace	18	Dakota	30
blanket	39	death	7
boll	12	degree	9
Booker	11	dip	19
British	21	earn	59
buffalo	30	else	8
built	34	equipment	35
businessmen	17	Europe	52
buzz	48	exact	22
Canadian	22	excitement	50
canoe	33	expedition	34
captain	30	explore	33
Carver	7	famous	7
Charbonneau	30	fell	31

62